FIRST KISSES

A Play in Two Acts

by
Jay D. Hanagan

SAMUEL FRENCH, INC.

45 West 25th Street   7623 Sunset Boulevard
NEW YORK 10010   HOLLYWOOD 90046
LONDON   *TORONTO*

ISBN 0 573 63374 6   Printed in U.S.A.   #8586

IMPORTANT BILLING AND CREDIT REQUIREMENTS

All producers of **FIRST KISSES** must give credit to the Author of the Play in all programs distributed in connection with performances of the Play, and in all instances in which the title of the Play appears for the purposes of advertising, publicizing or otherwise exploiting the Play and /or a production. The name of the Author must appear on a separate line on which no other name appears, immediately following the title and must appear in size of type not less than fifty percent of the size of the title type.

FIRST KISSES was initially a workshop production using multiple actors playing the two roles by the Gatesinger Company Ltd. under the working title "When I'm Kissing You" on January 31st, 2003 with John L' Hommedieu directing.

FIRST KISSES was presented as a reading by the Dayton Playhouse as a finalist at the 13th Annual Festival of New Works, Futurefest 2003, on July 26th, 2003. David Seyer was the Executive Director, and the production was directed by Fran Pesch with the following cast:

JOHN	David Mort
MARY	Annie Pesch
NARRATOR	Jackie Engle

FIRST KISSES was the winner of the Wichita Falls, Texas Backdoor Theatre's 20th Annual New Play Project on August 27, 2004 and was directed by Linda Bates with the following cast:

JOHN (age 11)	Brent Deed
MARY (age 11)	Emily Clements
JOHN (age 15,17,21)	Ryan Arnold
MARY (age 15,17,21)	Abigail Clements
JOHN (age 32,42,52)	Jim Sernoe
MARY (age 32,42,52)	Delight Clements
JOHN (age 72)	Patrick Jackson
MARY (age 72)	Roma Prassel

CHARACTERS

JOHN   A boy who becomes a man.
MARY   A girl who becomes a woman.

SCENE

In a small town. Between two properties, by a shack in the woods.

TIME

Today. Early October.

PLAYWRIGHT'S NOTES

This play was originally conceived to be played by two actors, assuming the roles of the characters as they age throughout the play. However, it is quite possible to have as few as two or as many as sixteen actors (two actors per scene), depending on your desires and resources. For example, eleven year-olds could play Act I, Scene One, and seventy year-olds could play Act II, Scene Five, and so fourth.

Also, the narration, which is to be integrated into the scene changes, not performed separately, at the beginning of various scenes can be performed live, or canned by the characters at what ever age you choose. Or be eliminated entirely.

In between scenes, there may be slides (or any presentation) shown of JOHN and MARY, depicting the years that had passed.

FIRST KISSES is for Elaine.

ACT I

Scene 1

(There is an old shed in the woods, center stage, that separate two properties. It has a platform type front porch with a roof supported by two beams at either end. The shed itself has been obviously abandoned for many years, and it shows. It is a secluded spot, not often visited. The property on either side of the shed belongs to the boy's family [stage left] or the girl's family [stage right]. Even though this is not the deep woods, the streets and houses cannot be readily seen. All the action of the play takes place here, in various seasons and years, as the boy and the girl grow up. AT RISE: We see the shed, center stage. JOHN ENTERS from s.l. He is eleven years of age. He is wearing a T-shirt, a light jacket, opened, and blue jeans. It is early October, on a pleasant and sunny Sunday, around noon. He is carrying a small backpack with a sack lunch and soda inside, as well as other items as we shall soon discover. He sits on the right corner of the porch as he starts to unpack his lunch and soda [which he will eat and drink through dialogue] as he looks appreciatively around him. He then addresses the audience...)

JOHN. A new family moved into town this week. Mom says they used to live here about seven or eight years ago and that I used to play with their kid. A girl. Well, I don't think so. Girls aren't a whole lot of fun to play with, you know what I mean? Worse yet, she said when we were little, they used to give us our baths together! How gross is that? Thank gosh I don't remember any of that or I'd have nightmares for sure. But you know sumptin', there's this new girl in my grade at school and she's kinda pretty... for a girl, and if it's the same girl, then she sure has aged good. *(Stands and wipes his hands on his pants.)* This is my secret place. *(Indicating the shed.)* I think this must have been used by some kind of criminals like bank robbers. Yeah, bank robbers. And they stashed their loot somewhere around here. And someday, I'm gonna find it. I only hope the robbers don't come back. You know what I mean? Anyhow, I was gonna tell some of my friends about this place, but I changed my mind. 'Cause if I tell 'em, then it wouldn't be a secret place anymore. *(We hear a twig snap.)* What was that? *(Listens a bit.)* The robbers? *(Quietly.)* Hell-ooo-oo. I'd better make sure no one is out there. You can't be too careful. *(EXITS s.l.)*

(MARY ENTERS from s.r. She is a pretty girl also eleven years old. She has shoulder length hair. She obviously did not pick out her clothing as she is wearing a dress that is perfect for a six year old, but not for our 'mature' eleven year old. It comes with a white button down sweater, which she has unbuttoned. She is also wearing dress shoes and white knee socks —how humiliating!—. The ensemble is a little scuffed and dirty from hiking in these woods. As she enters, she sees the shed, but does not yet notice the backpack. She addresses the audience.)

MARY. Well, look at this. An old shed or something. I wonder what was here. A tiny farmhouse? Yes. A tiny little farmhouse where the mother worked all day baking and cleaning and cooking and mending while the father worked all day in the fields... *(Pointing off left.)* over there before they put up all those houses... plowing and

FIRST KISSES

digging and sowing and harvesting so they could sell what little they grew at the market so they could buy more seeds and tools and cloth *(Getting louder.)* so the mother could make stupid dresses for the daughter to wear so she can look nice at church so then the mother and father can say to the daughter to go play with her new friends but she's eleven and she doesn't play and all her friends are back home and I don't know any of these people and what were they thinking!? *(Calm again.)* Yes, that's what this is. An old tiny one room farmhouse. *(She paces a bit and looks off s.l. and sees JOHN's house through the trees.)* That must be the house Mom and Papa were talking about. They said the people there were good friends with them when we lived here before. I guess I was too young to remember much from then. They said they were happy we were moving back home. But this isn't home to me. I guess when we lived here before I used to play with some little boy there, and that they used to give us our baths together. I could just die! *(She notices the backpack.)* Uh-oh. Someone's here on our property. *(Thinking.)* You know, there was a boy at church today that I'd seen at school and he was kind of cute. *(Sits on the porch next to the backpack.)* If he's the one who lives over there, then maybe this backpack is his. *(She starts to look inside.)* Why would anyone carry a shoe box around?! *(A twig snaps.)* What was that? *(A beat; quietly.)* Hell-ooo-oo.

(MARY hides behind the shed, eventually peeking out from the left side. JOHN ENTERS from s.l.)

JOHN. Surveillance of the area is complete. There's nobody around for miles. My secret spot is secure. No older kids, no grown-ups and no girls.

(MARY reacts to this, stepping out from cover, mouth open, fists on

hips. She quickly realizes she's exposed and ducks back. JOHN looks to MARY's house.)

JOHN. *(Contd.)* I have to keep a close eye on the enemy camp over there. There may be a border dispute.

(MARY starts waving her arms around at a mosquito. She then slaps her arm, which JOHN hears. JOHN then moves to investigate. MARY goes around the back as it appears JOHN follows, but he reappears very soon from the same side and leans against the corner support post. We then see MARY emerge from the other side, constantly checking her back, so that she does not at first see JOHN. As she rounds the corner, she turns around and sees him and is of course startled.)

MARY. Oh!

JOHN. Lost sumptin'?

MARY. *(As she tries to regain her composure.)* No. No I didn't.

JOHN. 'Cause you're on private property you know.

MARY. No. I didn't know. I mean I did know. My parents own this.

JOHN. Well, my parents said we own this, so I own it, which means you've got to beat it!

MARY. Me?! You beat it!

JOHN. Me?! I'm not goin' anywhere!

MARY. *(Sitting on the porch.)* Neither am I.

JOHN. Get outta here or I'll-

MARY. *(Stands.)* Or you'll what?!

JOHN. *(Not sure what he can do - he takes a step towards her, but then backs off. He looks around and tries but fails again.)* Look, I'm tellin' ya ya gotta go. This is my secret place.

MARY. "Secret place"?

FIRST KISSES

JOHN. *(Knowing he's blown it.)* I... I...

MARY *(Singsong.)* It's not a se-cret a-ny mo-ore!

JOHN. Aw, come on! Give me a break!

MARY. My name's Mary. What's yours? Or is it a secret?

JOHN. It's not a secret.

MARY. Then what is it?

JOHN. *(Relents.)* My name is John. Look, I found this place first.

MARY. So?

JOHN. *(Back to square one... he can't argue with that.)* Come on!

MARY. Tell you what. I need a secret place too. So this can be your secret place and it can be mine.

JOHN. There's no way I'm sharin' my place with any dumb g-

MARY. *(Spitting on the palm of her hand, then holding it out to him.)* What do you say? Is it a deal?

JOHN. Hey! Where'd you learn to do that?

MARY. What?

JOHN. That! *(The spitting on her hand.)*

MARY. Oh that. My papa. He teaches me a lot of cool stuff. I think I was supposed to be a boy.

JOHN. You don't look like no boy. Not in that thing!

MARY. *(Making a fist.)* You got a problem with this?

JOHN. I don't got a problem if you don't.

MARY. Well I don't! *(Yes she does.)* You live over there?

(Motioning towards his house off left.)

JOHN. Yeah. You live there?

(Motioning towards her house off right. At this point, they're starting to confirm who the other is.)

MARY. Yes. Hey, you're not...
JOHN. You mean you're the one...
MARY. We used to...
JOHN. Our parents used to...
MARY. In the bathtub...

(Both shudder at the thought, then start to eye each other, getting caught by the other looking, both totally embarrassed by now.)

JOHN. I don't feel so hot. This has been a lousy day.

MARY. How come?

JOHN. *(Snapping.)* None of your business! *(Thinks for a second.)* Okay. Here's the rules. It can be both our secret place, but whoever gets here first has first dibs and can tell the other to scram.

MARY. Okay. But only for a half hour. Then they gotta share.

JOHN. And no sneakin' around spyin'.

MARY. Okay.

JOHN. And no tellin' anyone!

MARY. I said okay!

JOHN. *(Spitting on the palm of his hand.)* Deal?

MARY. *(She does likewise as they shake hands.)* Deal.

JOHN. *(After a beat.)* You're okay. For a girl.

MARY. Yeah?

JOHN. Even when you look like that.

MARY. Hey! I didn't pick out this dress!

JOHN. I'm not talkin' 'bout no dress.

MARY. You're not?

JOHN. Nope.

MARY. What are you talkin' about then?

JOHN. I can't tell you.

MARY. Why not?

FIRST KISSES

JOHN. 'Cause it's a secret!

MARY. You tell me or I'll-

JOHN. Or you'll what?

MARY. *(Now she has the same problem JOHN had earlier.)*
I'll... I'll... oh come on!

JOHN. Where we goin'?

MARY. Tell me.

JOHN. Why?

MARY. Because.

JOHN. Because why?

MARY. All right then... don't.

JOHN. I won't.

MARY. I don't wanna know.

JOHN. Good, 'cause I don't wanna tell you.

MARY. Tell me!

JOHN. *(Sing song.)* I got a se-cret. I got a se-cret!

MARY. Please?

JOHN. Ask nice.

MARY. That was nice.

JOHN. Try again.

MARY. Pleeeeeeeease?

JOHN. Okay. But you're not gonna like it.

MARY. I don't care!

JOHN. Okay. You got a big ol' honkin' bugger hangin' out your
nose.

MARY. *(Checking immediately.)* I do not!

JOHN. Whoops! It just went back in again.

MARY. Did not!

JOHN. *(Pointing.)* There it is again!

MARY. Where?!

JOHN. There! *(He starts laughing, and after a beat so does she.
He got her and she knows it. As their laughter dies down-)* So your

dad thought you were a boy?

MARY. My papa. I call him my papa. No, it's just that I got an older sister, she's fifteen, and I think that when I was born, he was kind of hopin' for a boy.

JOHN. Well sure. Why not?

MARY. He's really great though. We go to ball games and fishing and stuff.

JOHN. Yeah? You fish? I go fishing all the time. You bait your own hook?

MARY. Sure.

JOHN. Your papa doesn't do it for you?

MARY. I've been baiting my own hook since I was two.

JOHN. That's pretty cool.

MARY. Thanks. Now what?

JOHN. You're outta here.

MARY. How come?

JOHN. 'Cause we made a deal!

MARY. Okay, okay! *(turns to go, stops after a couple of steps and turns back around.)* Have you ever kissed a girl?

JOHN. What!?!

MARY. Never mind. It's just that my sister is all boy crazy now and wants to kiss this boy and that boy and I don't think she's ever kissed any boy. *(Shrugs.)* I was just wondering what the big deal was, that's all.

JOHN. Are you going now?

MARY. You know what? She said sometimes when a boy and a girl kiss, they do it by putting their tongues inside each other's mouths.

JOHN. Ugh! Oh! Gross! Ew! Put a girl's tongue in my mouth? I'd rather eat live worms than do that! Are you sick or sumptin'?

MARY. My sister said it. I don't know.

JOHN. Get outta here before I puke!

FIRST KISSES

MARY. Okay, okay. I'm going. But I'll be back in half an hour.

JOHN. No sooner or you have to start over.

MARY.Okay. I said I'm going. Later.

JOHN. Yeah yeah, later.

MARY. *(Going slowly.)* See you later.

(JOHN ignores her as she EXITS s.r. He takes a small shoe box out of his backpack . He holds it very carefully as he looks around to make sure he's not being observed. He sets the box down and takes a small gardening trowel out of his backpack. He takes off his jacket and gets down on his knees and starts to dig a hole at the left corner of the porch. MARY can now be seen by us peering around the right corner of the shed, observing.)

JOHN. *(To the shoe box, or what's in it.)* I think you'll like it here. It's really quiet. I know how loud noises make you nervous. *(He digs some more as he talks. He does not notice MARY.)* You've been a really good friend, and I really tried to take good care of you. *(He stops digging and opens the box and looks inside.)* You've got your seed and some lettuce? Good. *(He puts the cover back on, puts the box in the hole and starts covering it up. He also starts choking up a bit as he talks. This is very sad for him.)* You always listened when I needed someone to talk to. You were always happy to see me. You were the best friend a guy could ever have. *(He pulls a couple of flower bulbs from the backpack, plants them, then covers everything up.)* Mom said these bulbs will grow into real pretty flowers every spring. I promise I'll visit a lot. *(Really holding back the tears now.)* And maybe we can talk. I know dad says you were only a hamster...

MARY. *(Despite herself.)* A hamster?!

JOHN. *(Jumping up, wiping away his tears.)* Hey! What are you doing here? We made a deal!

FIRST KISSES

MARY. *(Approaching JOHN.)* You're crying because your pet hamster died?

JOHN. I'm not crying! *(Wiping his eyes.)* And you broke your promise!

MARY. *(As she walks up to him.)* But that is so nice that you cry for your dead hamster.

(She gives him a quick kiss on the cheek, which he quickly wipes off.)

JOHN. *(Very embarrassed, stepping away.)* You broke your promise! And I'm not crying about some dumb ol' hamster. Stupid thing dies after only two years. What good are they? Running around on the stupid wheel... *(Trying not to cry some more, but angry now.)* You broke your promise!

MARY. I - I'm sorry. I really am. I didn't mean to... I'll go now.
JOHN. *(Shouting.)* Go on!
MARY. I'm going. I'm sorry.

(She turns and runs off s.r.)

JOHN. *(Shouting after her.)*Who cares! *(JOHN checks the grave, then goes to his backpack and pulls out a canteen filled with water. He carefully pours water on the grave for the bulbs. He stands and brushes the dirt from his jeans. He then bows his head, looks up once more to make sure she's really gone, bows his head and folds his hands together for prayer.)* God. Please watch over my friend, Samster the Hamster. He was really nice, and I'd much rather kiss any hamster right on his lips than to have a girl put her tongue in my mouth. Amen. *(He packs up his things and puts them back into his backpack. He then sits on the porch and addresses the audience.)*

FIRST KISSES

Dumb ol' girl. Makin' fun of me. Breakin' a promise. I hope she don't come back. Ever. *(Kicks some dirt and looks for her.)* Well I'm waitin' right here to see that she don't. And if she does come back and it's not a half hour yet, I'll make her go and start over again. *(He gets up, paces for a minute, then sits back down at the right edge of the porch. He takes his jacket and covers himself up like it was a blanket - obviously it's been a long long day for him - as he starts to fall asleep.)* Dumb ol' girl. I'm waitin'.. right... here...

(MARY ENTERS from s.r. She's carrying a small shoe box, much the same as JOHN's. She's changed her clothes, as she's now wearing jeans and a plaid flannel shirt. Her hair is in a pony tail.)

MARY. *(To the audience.)* It's been over an hour since I left. I hope he likes this. *(Indicating the box.)* I really am sorry. Any boy who feels that way about a hamster... *(Looking at JOHN.)*...he's just the nicest boy. *(She walks towards JOHN, looks at him and then looks at the audience and points to him, as if to say 'Aww. Isn't he cute?'. She then gently nudges him.)* John? *(Nudge.)* John?
JOHN. Huh? *(Waking up.)* What? What are you doing here?
MARY. *(Holding out the box.)* I brought you this.
JOHN. What is it?
MARY. It's for you. I wasn't laughing at you. Really I wasn't.
JOHN. I don't care.
MARY. Well, anyway, I got this for you. To say I'm sorry.

(She hands him the box, he takes it.)

JOHN. What's in it? *(About to shake the box.)*
MARY. No - no! Don't shake it!
JOHN. Why not?
MARY. Open it.

JOHN. *(Opening the box and looking in.)* What is this... a gag?

MARY. No, it's a hamster.

JOHN. Where'd you get it?

MARY. I got it. For you.

JOHN. *(Suspiciously.)* Why?

MARY. Like I told you. To say I'm sorry. You must have taken real good care of your hamster for him to live for two years. That's a long time for a hamster.

JOHN. You know about hamsters? Most girls won't even touch one you know.

MARY. I know.

JOHN. And they're real friendly.

MARY. I know. What was your hamster's name?

JOHN. *(About to answer her, but realizes how silly it's going to sound.)* I forget.

MARY. You did not.

JOHN. Did too.

MARY. His name either rhymed with hamster or started with an "h". Which was it?

JOHN. *(Sheepishly.)* Samster.

MARY. "Samster"? That's so sweet!

JOHN. It is not sweet, and if you tell anybody I'll knock your block off!

MARY. I won't tell anybody. Why would I? *(A beat.)* Her name is Harriet.

JOHN. Her name?

MARY. Umm... the person at the store said it was a girl hamster, so I thought Harriet would be a nice name-

JOHN. You got me a girl hamster?

MARY. It's no big deal. Besides, you probably wouldn't have been able to tell the difference if I hadn't told ya.

JOHN. Sure I would.

FIRST KISSES

MARY. *(Prove it.)* How?

JOHN. Just *(Reaches inside the box.)* turn him over.

MARY. She likes her belly rubbed.

JOHN. How do you know?

MARY. Uh, just guessing. I read it in a book somewhere. *(They both reach in the box to check out the hamster.)* Well? Boy or girl?

JOHN. *(He can't tell.)* Uh - you're right. It's a girl.

MARY. I think she likes you.

JOHN. Yeah?

MARY. 'Cause you're so gentle.

JOHN. Well, they're just little you know.

MARY. I know.

JOHN. Well, thanks. I'll have to clean out Samster's cage first. To get rid of his smell.

MARY. I could help.

JOHN. Yeah? Okay. 'Cause I like- I mean Harriet likes you too. *(A beat as they both fiddle with Harriet some more.)* You know how you said how you wouldn't tell nobody 'bout Samster or anything?

MARY. Yeah...

JOHN. Did you mean it?

MARY. Well yeah! If I tell you any secrets, you wouldn't tell anyone, would you?

JOHN. Heck no! I'm no snitch!

MARY. Because I really need a friend I can talk to. And you know how girls are.

JOHN. *(Agreeing with her.)* Yeah.

MARY. So, it's a deal?

JOHN. *(Setting down the box.)* Sure it's a deal. *(He spits on his hand and holds it out. MARY however, leans over, and kisses him quickly on the lips. She pulls back and they look at each other. MARY is smiling and JOHN looks a little pleased but mostly in shock. MARY leans in for another kiss. This time, she cups his face in her hands as*

FIRST KISSES

we see JOHN's eyes get real wide. As he tries to get away, he bumps his head against the post as he struggles to back off.) You put your tongue in my mouth! Eww! Ick! Ick! *(He tries first to clean his tongue by wiping it on the sleeves of his shirt.)* Where's the hamster?! I gotta kiss the hamster! *(He picks up the box and sticks his head in to kiss Harriet but-)* Ow! She bit me on the nose!

MARY. Well you scared her.

JOHN. I scared her? *(He gets down on all four's.)*

JOHN. *(Contd.)* Where's a worm? - there's gotta be a worm. I gotta eat a worm to get this taste outta my mouth!

MARY. *(More to herself.)* I don't see what all the fuss was about. *(Meaning not this fuss but the fuss her sister makes.)* It was nothing great. But I didn't think it was gross or anything. Did you think it was gross?

JOHN. A worm! I gotta find a worm! Ick! Ick! *(To MARY.)* I was just starting to like you and then you ruined it!

MARY. Really? You like me?

JOHN. *(Still looking for worms.)* Ick. Ugh. Eww.

MARY. *(Pleased.)* Well, I've got to go now. Take good care of Harriet for me. *(Starts to back away.)* I'm sorry I made you want to eat worms. Thanks.

JOHN. *(Looks up, still peeved.)* Thanks for what?

MARY. Thanks for being my new friend. And I promise to keep our secrets. I promise. G'bye. *(She runs off right.)*

JOHN. *(Getting up and looking after her.)* G'bye. *(Then yells off right.)* And thanks for the hamster. I'll take good care of her. Hey! You were gonna help me clean her cage. *(He picks up the box and runs off right after her.)* Hey! Wait up!

End of Scene

FIRST KISSES

Scene Two

(The same place, about three and a half years later in May. It is about three in the afternoon and warm for early May. MARY and JOHN are both fourteen. The flowers that were planted earlier appear to be blooming again. We also notice a second grave with like flowers next to it. Here lies Harriet Hamster.)

NARRATOR. *(O.S.)* And so heroes grow as heroes will do, which can be of great comfort to heroes like you. And the flowers still bloom that remind us of things like Spring, as the cool of an autumn turns to warmth... call it May, three and some years e're they kissed that first day. From elev'n to fourteen a lifetime of growing, or so it must seem... they grow without knowing. And so heroes grow, as heroes must do...

(MARY ENTERS from the right. She is wearing a sleeveless top and hiking shorts. She has on comfortable white sneakers and white ankle socks. Her hair is in a ponytail. She is carrying a large canvas bag. She paces and stops, back and forth as she keeps looking at her watch.)

MARY. He's late. Come on! I don't have all day. *(To the audience.)* Mom and Papa moved back here three or four years ago 'cause Papa got a better job here, and Mom always liked living here. *(Glances again at her watch.)* He's never late. I'm always late, but he's never late. Mom's a substitute teacher, and so it was easy for her to get a job here and there. They like her. Everyone likes my mom. Anyway, Papa just got laid off from work. So now money's tight. My English teacher would call that 'ironic'. So here I am, my first year in high school and my sister's first year in college. College equals tuition which equals no money for yours truly. *(Looks at her watch again.)* Where is he? So anyway, like I was sayin', here I am a high school freshman, with absolutely no chance of goin' to the senior prom when out of the blue pops Rich Benson. Yes, the Rich Benson. Senior. 'B.M.O.C.' as my papa would say. So anyway, Rich and his girlfriend, Ju-lee-ah-nah got into a fight and split up. Rich knows me from band right?, and BINGO! I'm going to the prom. But here's the problem. No money equals no dress. And no dress means no prom. *(Looks at her watch.)* Where is he? *(JOHN ENTERS from the left. His hands are in his jeans pockets. He's also wearing a clean t shirt and worn sneakers. His head is down as he walks. His mind is clearly someplace else.)* Where have you been?! You're late!

JOHN. Huh? Oh. Sorry, I forgot.

MARY. You forgot? You forgot? *(JOHN sits on the porch and leans back on his hands, staring out at nothing in particular. MARY finally picks up that all is not right.)* Hey, what's the matter? Report cards aren't due for another few weeks. Ha ha. *(Punches him kiddingly on the shoulder.)*

JOHN. *(Not making eye contact.)* My mom has cancer.

MARY. *(Stunned.)* What? Are they sure? *(JOHN nods, still not making eye contact.)* Well... well, what kind? Is she going to be okay? *(She sits next to him.)*

JOHN. She hadn't been feeling too good for a while. I knew that. Then she goes to the doctor's... goes to the hospital for an operation while I'm at school. They didn't even tell me!

MARY. I can't believe it. I'm so sorry.

JOHN. They should have told me!

MARY. I know.

JOHN. *(Getting more upset.)* I'm fourteen years old. I'm not a kid.

MARY. I know.

JOHN. What if she had died?

FIRST KISSES

MARY. She'll be fine. You know she'll be fine.

JOHN. *(Quieter.)* She could have died.

MARY. *(Patting and rubbing his back with one hand.)* She'll be okay. They just didn't want you to worry. She'll be okay. You'll see. You'll visit her soon and you'll know.

JOHN. You think?

MARY. Sure.

JOHN. They should have told me.

MARY. They should have told you.

(She reaches out for a hug. JOHN smiles slightly and they hug.)

JOHN. So what am I late for anyway?

MARY. Nothing. Nothing really.

JOHN. It must have been something. Come on. Help me get my mind off things.

MARY. That's okay. Everything doesn't always have to be about me you know. *(JOHN gives her an "Oh really?" look.)* Okay, sometimes it does have to be about me.

JOHN. So what's goin' on?

MARY. It's not important.

JOHN. Okay, never mind.

MARY. Okay, if you insist. As you know, I'm going to be going to the senior prom...

JOHN. Not the prom again!

MARY. ... with Rich Benson.

JOHN. So I've heard.

MARY. But I have no dress.

JOHN. And heard.

MARY. And I can't go to the prom without a dress.

JOHN. And heard.

FIRST KISSES

MARY. My Mom says, "Now Mary, money's tight right now, and your sister's in college..."

JOHN. And heard.

MARY. *(Shushes him!)* It's always about my sister, you know. *(JOHN opens his mouth to speak.)* Don't say it! But it's a prom! Mom says we can buy a used dress, and I'm like oh that's great. Everyone can say something like "Oh that dress looks just as nice on you as it did on so-and-so last year." Or "is that dress back in style so soon?"

JOHN. They just don't think do they?

MARY. Don't be smart. So my papa comes up to me and says "I feel like an ice cream cone. Want to come with me?"

JOHN. So you got ice cream.

MARY. He said he was very sorry we couldn't afford a dress just now. The credit cards are all maxed out and we just don't have the money. But he says my Mom has some pretty material at home and that she wants to make me a dress herself.

JOHN. Hey! That'll be nice! Problem solved!

MARY. Are you kidding? Anyway, Papa must have seen the look of horror on my face. He said that my Mom's a real good sower, he said 'sower', he's such a papa. Anyway, she won't start work on it until I give my okay. He asks me if I'll let her do this for me. He said it would mean a lot to her.

JOHN. That's not playin' fair.

MARY. Tell me! So I said okay. Then he said I should ask her and to be real enthusiastic about it. So I did and she did *(Holds up the bag.)* and here it is.

JOHN. Good.

MARY. But now I don't know what it's gonna look like on me, so I need your help.

JOHN. *(States firmly.)* Oh no! I am not going to try on that dress.

MARY. I don't want you to try it on. I want to try it on and I

FIRST KISSES

want you to tell me how hideous I look in it.

JOHN. Oh, I can do that easy.

MARY. And quick. My mother's waiting. *(JOHN stares at her for a beat.)* She thinks I'm in my room.

JOHN. Oh.

MARY. I'm going inside the shack to change. Do not peek.

JOHN. Who wants to peek? I just had lunch.

MARY. Ha ha.

JOHN. Hurry up. I want to visit my mom.

MARY. *(Happy to see JOHN's ready to see his mom.)* Good. I'll hurry. *(She goes into the shack.)*

JOHN. *(To the audience.)* I don't have the heart to tell her that Rich and Julianna are probably going to get back together before the prom. That's what everyone is saying anyway. So that's gonna leave her out. So when she comes out, I'll just tell her how awful she looks and she'll say she's not goin' and that should do it.

MARY. *(From inside the shack.)* Okay. Here goes. Remember, be honest. *(She comes out of the shack, her eyes shut. She still has on her sneakers and her hair is still in the pony tail. Other than that, she is beautiful. It is a floor length dress so she has to stand on tip toes and hike it up a bit when she walks. It is very fashionable and up to date. It is not at all tight, but still shows she's starting to get her figure. JOHN is speechless. He opens his mouth but nothing comes out. He just stares. This is probably the first time he has seen her as a girl other than as a friend.)* Well? *(Silence.)* John? *(She opens her eyes.)* John!

JOHN. You're a girl.

MARY. I know that! *(A beat.)* Really?

JOHN. Do you know what you look like?

MARY. No. Is it awful? I've been too afraid to look.

JOHN. You're real pretty.

MARY. What?

JOHN. *(Snapping out of it.)* The dress. The dress is pretty. You look okay. Your mom did a nice job. You ought to go see for yourself.

MARY. Really? You think so? *(Looking.)* It does look kind of nice. I've got to go home and look in the mirror.

(She starts off right.)

JOHN. Wait! You don't want to hike home in that!

MARY. *(Calling as she EXITS.)* I'll be right back.

JOHN *(To himself.)* I am such a jerk! When did she start looking like that? *(To the audience.)* Did you see her? Did you know? You could have warned me. *(To himself, looking off at her.)* Oh sister, I thought she was a sister but she's no sister. *(To the audience.)* She was gone for quite a while. She said she'd be right back. I wish she'd hurry up. I really want to see my mom. All I can say is that Rich better not hurt her or I'll...

(MARY ENTERS running - as best she can. Her hair is down and messy, but what's worse is, her dress is torn, just a little near the left shoulder, but it is enough. The dress is ruined. She is frightened, embarrassed, angry and out of breath, trying not to cry.)

JOHN. Mary! What happened?

MARY. *(Pointing off; very quickly.)* They're over there, laughing- Julianna's brother- he and some other big jerk they grabbed me- !

JOHN. What?! Who?! Slow down!

MARY. *(Still very upset.)* Julianna's brother. He said "What are you all dressed up for?" I told them to get out of my way, but he grabbed me. They grabbed me!

FIRST KISSES

JOHN. Easy, take it easy. Are you okay?

MARY. They said if Julianna wasn't going with Rich to the dance then no one was going with Rich, and they started grabbing at me and *(Just noticing the tear.)* Oh! They tore my dress. They tore it! It's ruined! And my mom worked so hard on it and it was beautiful and you said I was pretty and now it's ruined.

JOHN. *(Not knowing what to do. Keeps taking a step or two off towards the right as he speaks to the audience.)* I can't believe this. First my mom's sick and my parents treat me like I'm some dumb kid, and then these jerks make my best friend cry. And I know I'm about to get the snot kicked out of me, but I don't care. *(Calling off right.)* Hey you! Assholes! Yeah, I'm talkin' to you! *(EXITS right.)*

MARY. John, don't! *(We hear fighting from off right.)* Oh no! John! Be careful! *(She doesn't know what to do... she can't help, because of the dress. We then hear the fighting stop. JOHN REEN-TERS from the right. His shirt is torn, his pants scuffed. He has what looks to be a nice shiner coming. There's blood around his lip and nose. He is holding his hand. For some reason, she finds this act of heroism amusing.)* Oh my. Are you okay?

JOHN. I think I broke my hand. *(MARY suppresses a giggle.)* You're laughing?

MARY. My hero.

JOHN. Cut it out.

MARY. I'm sorry. I just never had anyone come to my rescue before.

JOHN. Well no wonder if that's how you're going to act.

MARY. It was really sweet.

JOHN. I break my hand and she says it's sweet.

MARY. *(Still trying not to laugh.)* I'm sorry. So. Who won the fight?

JOHN. *(With false bravado.)* Let's just say that one of them's not going to be eating any solid food for quite a while. The other coward took off before I was finished with him.

    MARY. You shouldn't have done it. It wasn't worth it.

    JOHN. It was worth it to me. Besides. I didn't know what else to do. You were crying.

    MARY. *(Sadly.)* I guess I'm not going to the prom now.

    JOHN. That's okay. You'd have just gone and gotten everyone mad at you 'cause you'd have been the prettiest one there with that dress.

    MARY. You really think so?

    JOHN. Sure.

    MARY. My mom will be so hurt that I ruined her dress. She worked so hard on it.

    JOHN. Tell her you loved it. That's all she wants to hear anyway.

    MARY. I wish she could have seen me in it. *(A beat.)* Did you really think I was pretty?

    JOHN. *(A little embarrassed.)* Oh. Yeah. I guess.

    MARY. I guess that's all I needed to know. Doesn't really seem worth it now.

    JOHN. *(Sincerely.)* It was worth it.

(MARY walks up to JOHN and kisses him.)

    MARY. Let me change here, then you can get a clean shirt, and we can visit your mom.

    JOHN. Wear the dress so she can see you in it.

    MARY. It's torn.

    JOHN. She won't care.

(MARY picks up her other clothes, and as the two walk off left, arm in arm...)

FIRST KISSES

MARY. Did you really beat those two bullies up?

JOHN. Are you kidding me? Did you see the size of them?

MARY. Are you all right?

JOHN. Let's just say I'm not going to be eating any solid food for a while.

MARY. *(Squeezing his arm, laughing.)* My hero.

(Lights fade to blackout.)

End of Scene

Scene Three

(The scene is three years and three months later; they are seventeen about to turn eighteen. It is August. The two graves still have flowers on them.)

NARRATOR. *(O.S.)* Finality of change, oxymoron you say? Not really. Consider. As heroes their way. Can't undo what's been done, can't undo what's been said, can't go back to before... why not stand straight ahead? The future is lonely when faced all alone, the past is a myst'ry... future pasts are unknown. Warm August breezes three some years from the past, young adults as they may, stronger friends since seen last. Heroes love other heroes, kindred spirits of rhyme, holding tight to one 'nother... facing both sides of time.

(MARY is sitting on the porch, alone for the moment. She is wearing

shorts, a tank top and sandals. JOHN runs in from left. He is wearing jean shorts and a tee shirt, sneakers and no socks.)

JOHN. Oh good! It's still here!

MARY. For how long?

JOHN. I can't believe our fathers want to tear this down.

MARY. They said it isn't safe. That if any little kids from the neighborhood wandered by, that it might collapse and hurt them.

JOHN. Nah, never happen. Hey wait a minute. They're more concerned with neighbor kids than with us?

MARY. I don't think they know we come out here.

JOHN. *(Ignoring her.)* Sure, the whole thing can collapse on my head and who cares right?

MARY. Well now what are we going to do?

JOHN. What do you mean?

MARY. Our secret place may be violated. We'll have no place to go to. We'll be orphaned.

JOHN. *(To himself.)* And I never did find that stolen loot.

MARY. What? Stolen what?

JOHN. Huh? Oh, forget it. What do our dads know? Nobody could get hurt around this old shed. Look at it. It's solid. Nobody builds like this...*(He gives the side of the building a couple good smacks with his hand, whereas a two by four drops from the porch overhang)* ... anymore.

MARY. *(As they both sit on the porch.)* I'm going to miss this place. When I needed quiet to do homework, I'd come here. When I got mad at Mom or Papa, I'd come here. When I needed to find you, or have you find me, I'd come here. We've been coming here since we were kids.

JOHN. Well, we're not kids anymore.

MARY. You know what it is? A shelter. That's what it is.

JOHN. Oh grow up will you? You're awfully sentimental for an

FIRST KISSES

eighteen year old.

MARY. Almost eighteen. Next week.

JOHN. I know. We have the same birthday.

MARY. So happy birthday.

JOHN. Like brother and sister.

MARY. *(Quietly.)* Like brother and sister.

JOHN. *(To audience.)* Our parents met at the hospital that day. They said it was a full house.

MARY. *(To audience.)* We all kind of became roommates. *(To JOHN.)* Hey, with all the commotion at the hospital that day, do you think it's possible that we may have been switched at birth?

JOHN. I don't think that could have happened.

MARY. Sure, it could have happened! It happens all the time! Maybe we ended up with the wrong parents. We both have dark hair. We looked a lot alike. It could have happened.

JOHN. Except for one important thing.

MARY. What's that?

JOHN. You don't know.

MARY. No.

JOHN. Let's just say the difference puts me in an enviable position.

MARY. I have no idea what you're talking about.

JOHN. You'll either be tickled pink or very blue when you figure it out.

MARY. I hate it when you get like this.

JOHN. Dummy! It's obvious! I'm a boy and you're a girl! You think they wouldn't notice that?

MARY. So you noticed I'm a girl.

JOHN. There's no talking to you some days.

MARY. *(Beat.)* Let's fix the shack.

JOHN. What? You're nuts.

MARY. We have a couple of weeks before school starts. We can

FIRST KISSES

do this. *(Goes to pick up the two by four.)* Look. All it needs is a few nails and maybe replace some rotted stuff. We can do this- Ow! *(Drops the two by four.)*

JOHN. What happened?

MARY. I think I got a splinter.

JOHN. Let's see. *(Takes her hand.)* Hold still, I can see it. *(He keeps holding her hand with one hand while fishing around in his pocket with the other and pulls out one of those "Swiss army knives". He fiddles with the knife.)* Where are those tweezers? Okay. Hold still.

(He works to get the splinter under dialogue.)

MARY. Can you see okay?

JOHN. Yeah. *(Still working.)*

MARY. How's your mom doing? She just had a checkup didn't she?

JOHN. *(Still working.)* Yeah. Hold still. She's good. Still no sign of the cancer. She feels real good. Got it! *(Holds it up triumphantly.)*

MARY. Thanks. So what do you think? Going to help me fix this up, or do I have to do it myself.

JOHN. I still think you're nuts, but okay, let's do it.

MARY. Great! Let's get to work. *(She picks up the two by four, tosses it and...)* Ow!

JOHN. You did it again?

MARY. I think so. I can't see it 'though.

JOHN. *(Getting out his tweezers.)* Here, let me look. *(He takes her hand and looks.)* I can't see it either.

MARY. It's there, I can feel it.

JOHN. Okay, hold still. *(Still looking.)* Your dad settle into his new job yet?

FIRST KISSES

MARY. I guess so.

JOHN. This is what, his third job over the last couple of years?

MARY. Yes. Ow! Don't squeeze so hard.

JOHN. Sorry. My folks said he had a job offer from out of state, near your sister's college. You going to be moving soon?

MARY. Don't get me started on that! I absolutely refused to move anywhere! This is my senior year at high school and I'm not going to lose all my friends and have to make all new friends and graduate with a bunch of strangers! They said moving wouldn't kill me and I said staying wasn't going to kill them.

JOHN. So he turned down that job?

MARY. I guess. We're still here.

JOHN. It's just that... I still can't see anything... it's just that my folks said he really wanted that other job. They don't think he likes it where he is.

MARY. *(Pulling her hand away, walking a couple of steps away from him.)* Goes to show what you know. He likes it as well as anywhere.

JOHN. They say he's hardly home anymore, is he?

MARY. What are you saying, that I should have moved away?.

JOHN. No. It's just that, well, my folks are worried about him.

MARY. *(Crosses him.)* Tell your folks to mind their own business.

JOHN. *(Grabbing her as she passes.)* Hey, what's the matter with you?

MARY. *(Yanking her arm free.)* Nothing. I don't know. I feel a little funny. No, no nothing's the matter with me. Do you want to fix this stupid thing or what?

JOHN. *(Puzzled.)* Sure. I guess.

MARY. I'll go get some gloves so I don't get any more stupid splinters.

FIRST KISSES

(She EXITS s.r.)

JOHN. I'll go get some tools and nails. *(Calling off.)* I'll see you in a few minutes. *(He walks to s.l. And picks up two hammers, a saw and a bag of nails from just off left.; then to audience.)* I picked up some tools from home and some nails. I was gone and back within fifteen minutes. I waited for her for about another half an hour, but she never showed. Did I tick her off or something? I don't know. Anyway, I guessed she wasn't coming back, so I went home.

(The stage fades to darkness as a f.s. is on JOHN as he reaches just offstage for a battery lantern - and during this, MARY enters unseen and sits on the s.r. side of the porch staring off into nothing. The only light will be from the f.s. / lantern.)

JOHN. *(Contd.)* At home I found out why she didn't come back. I couldn't believe it. I wanted to go see her right away but my folks said to wait. Then the phone rang. I jumped a mile. After a short talk, my mom came back and told me Mary's mom didn't know where Mary was. *(JOHN crosses to where MARY is.)* I told Mom I'd find her. *(To MARY.)* I'm sorry to hear about your dad.
MARY. Thank you.
JOHN. You okay?
MARY. No.
JOHN. *(Sitting next to her, setting the lantern on the ground in front of them.)* I'm sorry.
MARY. You said that.
JOHN. How 'bout I walk you home.
MARY. Not yet.
JOHN. I think your mom's worried about you.
MARY. In a minute.
JOHN. How's your sister?

FIRST KISSES

MARY. Meg? She's a basket case. She's no help to mom at all.

JOHN. So let's you and I go back so you can help your mom.

MARY. She's screaming and crying and carrying on, just when mom needs her to be strong.

JOHN. So why are you sitting here? Come on, let's go.

MARY. I'm collecting my thoughts. I've got to show mom that I can take care of myself... that she doesn't need to worry about me.

JOHN. *(After a pause.)* So what happened?

MARY. Mom said he called home to say he'd be working late again. A half jour later she got another call... they found him slumped over his desk. Myocardial infarction. What kind of word is that? *(A beat.)* They said there wasn't anything they could have done... it was too massive. Somebody said maybe it was the stress *(Getting quieter.)* of the ... new ... job. *(Gasps as if just realizing something.)* Oh my God.

JOHN. What? What is it?

MARY. I killed my papa.

JOHN. What? Don't be ridiculous -

MARY. I did. I killed him. It was the stress. If we had moved he'd still be alive! It's all my fault!

JOHN. No! No it's not, you can't think that-

MARY. *(Stands and walks slightly towards home.)* They must hate me. My mother and sister must hate me! I can't go back now, I can't!

JOHN. *(Standing.)* Stop it Mary, just stop it. That's not true.

MARY. How could I have been so selfish?

JOHN. *(Going to her, taking her by her shoulders.)* Listen to me. You can't be playing 'what if's'. You didn't kill him. He died of a heart attack. *(Quieter.)* His heart... just stopped. *(Softly.)* It just stopped Mary. That's all. And it's no one's fault.

MARY. You should go now. Tell them I'll be back soon. It's not true, but tell them that anyway.

FIRST KISSES

JOHN. I'm not leaving you alone.

MARY. You have to. Those are the rules, remember? They've been the rules since we were kids.

JOHN. Forget the rules. Your mother needs you home. She doesn't need you strong and she doesn't need you brave. She just needs you home.

MARY. It's real easy for you, isn't it?. You've got two parents. You don't have to worry about money or college or... or food.

JOHN. I don't think you're going to starve-

MARY. How dare you!? Just who the hell do you think you are anyway?

JOHN. I didn't mean anything by it. I'm just trying to help.

MARY. You can't help me! Nobody can help me! Dead is dead! You want to help? Give me back my papa!

JOHN. Let's go back now.

MARY. There you go again! I am not a child. I do not need anyone to hold my hand.

JOHN. I'm sorry -

MARY. Stop saying that! I don't give a shit that you're sorry! And guess what? I'm sorry. I'm sorry that I don't have a father any more. I'm sorry my mother is a widow. My papa is dead. Why isn't your mother dead? She's the one who was sick! *(Abrupt silence as MARY realizes what she just said, and JOHN just stares at her.)* Oh my God. Oh my God I didn't say that. *(He looks away.)* I didn't mean it. I swear I didn't- *(Starting to tear up.)* He was my papa.

JOHN. I know.

MARY. *(Backing away.)* No! I said I was not going to do this. I will not cry. I can not let my mother see I've been crying.

JOHN. Crying's okay.

MARY. No it is not. It is not okay. Nothing will ever be oh-kay again!

JOHN. Let me walk you home.

FIRST KISSES

MARY. *(Shaking her head.)* No.

JOHN. You want to be strong? You want to be brave? Then prove it. Go home.

MARY. He was my papa.

(He holds her as she starts to cry on his shoulder.)

JOHN. I know.

MARY. *(Still crying.)* What am I going to do? What am I going to do? *(They stand there for a moment holding each other until she's through.)* Okay. Well, that was quite a scene, wasn't it? *(She wipes one of her eyes.)* I must look awful.

JOHN. *(Wipes away a tear from her other eye.)* You look beautiful.

(They look into each other's eyes for a moment, then without looking away or closing their eyes, they kiss.)

MARY. *(She says this as obviously matter of fact, and he responds in kind.)* I love you.

JOHN. I love you too.

MARY. Will you always be my best friend?

JOHN. You know it.

MARY. And keep my secrets?

JOHN. Let me walk you home. *(As they start off right...)*

Curtain. End of Act

FIRST KISSES

Act Two

Scene One

(It is three years and ten months later in June. They are both twenty-one, almost twenty-two, years old. We see that the shed is still standing. The flowers to the hamster graves are there and blooming. It is about two o'clock in the afternoon, and maybe a little cloudy. Lights up as JOHN is seen wearing a tuxedo, a little worse for wear. The tie is undone as is some of his dress shirt. He is carrying and drinking from a champagne bottle, and he is a little drunk. He is pacing back and forth muttering to himself. MARY sits on the porch with a bemused (if not amused) look on her face. Elbows resting on her knees, chin resting in her hands, watching him pace. She is wearing one of those hideous looking bridesmaid's dresses.)

MARY. And they said it wouldn't last. *(JOHN stops pacing and muttering just long enough to glare at MARY disdainfully, then continues.)* Sah-ree.*(She gets no other response from him. She smoothes and straightens out her dress and looks about for a bit.)* Look at me, a nice June afternoon, all dressed up with no where to go. Hey, you doing anything tonight? *(JOHN stops, his back turned to MARY. He slowly turns around and if looks could kill...)* Oh lighten up! So she dumped you. Big deal. Okay, she dumped you thirty minutes before you were to get married. It could have been worse, it could have

39

been thirty minutes after. You know, it took an awful lot of courage on her part to do what she did. Everything was set. The reception was paid for. Families were there. Marrying you just to make everyone else happy would have been wrong. You'd have both been miserable.

JOHN. *(Softening his stance, takes another swig. Note: The actor playing JOHN must remember he is drunk. Not all the dialogue is written phonetically to reflect that.)* You're right. *(He plops down next her with a heavy thud.)*

MARY. I am?

JOHN. You are.

(Offers her the bottle, which she takes.)

MARY. How 'bout that? *(Takes a swig.)* Oh! This is awful! *(Hands it back to him.)*

JOHN. I know. *(Takes another swig.)*

MARY. *(Putting her hand on his shoulder.)* This is for the best you know. You'd only been dating each other for four months. You hardly knew her.

JOHN. Oh, sure. We only liked the same things like movies, books 'n music. And she's not too bad on the eyes mind you. A relationship like that was doomed from the start.

MARY. Sometimes people turn out to be right for each other, and sometimes they don't.

JOHN. And you're the expert on who's right for who(m)? *(He has problems with the word(s) 'who(m)', neither sounds right to him.)*

MARY. You're only twenty-one. You need to finish college anyway.

JOHN. I'd have finished.

FIRST KISSES

(Now he has trouble with the word 'finished'.)

MARY. Sure, sure. How much have you had to drink?

JOHN. Just this little bit here.

MARY. That's good.

JOHN. *(Pointing.)* And that bottle there.

MARY. That's it?

JOHN. That's it.

MARY. Good.

JOHN. And that bottle wa-a-a-ay over there. *(Confidentially.)* That was my first.

MARY. First ever?

JOHN. No, no. *(Wait a beat.)* First ever what?

MARY. I think you're a little drunk.

JOHN. No-o-o. Well maybe. What do you think?

MARY. I think it's time I took you home. *(Stands and takes his arm.)*

JOHN. Let go of me you hussy. You're just trying to take advantage of me.

MARY. Oh for God's sake!

JOHN. *(Counting on his fingers.)* One. I am now on the rebound since I am no longer betrothed to um, betrothed to um...

MARY. Ellen.

JOHN. Who?

MARY. Your fiancée.

JOHN. I have no fiancée. *(He has trouble with the word 'fiancée'.)*

MARY. Fee-ahn-say.

JOHN. Fie-nance-ear.

MARY. Close enough.

JOHN. Who?

MARY. Ellen.

FIRST KISSES

JOHN. Ellen. A sweet girl. She said she loved me. Did you know that?

MARY. That was the rumor.

JOHN. Where was I?

MARY. When?

JOHN. I must be a little tipsy.

MARY. Oh really?

JOHN. Yes, really. That dress is starting to look good.

MARY. *(Pulling him up to his feet.)* So where were you?

JOHN. When?

MARY. Just now.

JOHN. Sitting and drinking.

MARY. Let's go.

JOHN. *(Counts on his fingers.)* And "B".

MARY. What?

JOHN. I just remembered where I left off. One was rebound. "B" is I'm a little wasted. That's why you're trying to take advantage of me.

MARY. I'll try to constrain myself.

JOHN. I should hope so. I'm very vun-er-a-ble right now. *(Sits down hard.)* Is the room spinning or is it me?

MARY. It's the room.

JOHN. It's spinning?

MARY. Uh-huh.

JOHN. I thought so.

MARY. Why don't you lie down?

JOHN. Good idea. *(Start to lie down, then sits right back up again.)* Not a good idea.

MARY. *(Very amused by all this.)* How come?

JOHN. The ground is spinning too.

MARY. Try putting your head between your knees.

FIRST KISSES

(JOHN starts to lower his head but loses his balance and almost falls forward. MARY catches him in time, and sits next to him.)

JOHN. You're just chuck full of good ideas aren't you?

MARY. Here, put your head on my lap. It's not spinning and I can hold your head so it won't spin.

JOHN. *(As he lowers his head)* I don't think this is going to work. *(As MARY strokes his hair.)* Hey, this is comfy. *(Sits up.)* You're not still trying to take advantage of me are you because one—

MARY. *(Lowering his head back.)* I promise I'm not trying to take advantage of you.

JOHN. This is very soft and sa-tin-ny. Did you know that?

MARY. Hmm-mm.

JOHN. I think I'm going to take a little nap now. It's been a lo-o-ng day. And before that it was a lo-o-ng night.

MARY. *(Gently.)* Shh.

JOHN. *(Echoing her.)* Shh. You're very comfortable. I have always found you to be very com-for-ta-ble.

MARY. Me too.

JOHN. You find you to be com-fort-a-ble too? *(He laughs at his little 'joke'.)* You wanna hear a secret?

MARY. Sure.

JOHN. I got dumped today.

MARY. So I heard.

JOHN. Who told?

MARY. It's kind of an open secret.

JOHN. You know what she said?

MARY. Who?

JOHN. Whats-her-name.

MARY. Ellen?

JOHN. Who?

MARY. What'd she say?

FIRST KISSES

JOHN. She said she loved me but she couldn't marry me. How's that for a kick in the nuts?

MARY. Sounds painful.

JOHN. It is. It's very painful. So's getting dumped, which is what I got.

MARY. If she loves you, why didn't she marry you?

JOHN. *(Starts to sit up, MARY keeps his head down.)* I asked her the very same thing. Do you know what she said?

MARY. No.

JOHN. Me neither. She said some bullshit thing about not resolving my feelings about others or some other horse shit thing like that. Did I say 'horse shit' or 'bullshit' earlier? I want to be consistent.

MARY. *(Worried now.)* What other feelings?

JOHN. Apparently, I'm not only in love with her, I'm in love with you.

MARY. *(Startled.)* You are?

JOHN. So you know what I told her? I told her "poppycock", only not in so many words. And she said, "Don't you 'poppycock' me!" *(Starts laughing.)* No she didn't. She said some horse bull thing about sometimes you get over your first love and sometimes you don't. She said she hoped she could. She kissed me here *(Pointing.)* on my lips and she was crying, and she turned and walked away. And I turned and walked the other way and found some really awful champagne and I walked and walked. How did you find me anyway?

MARY. *(Sadly, as she has been very affected by this.)* Oh, I don't know. Lucky guess.

JOHN. Because this is a secret place you know.

MARY. I know.

JOHN. Just so long as you know. You wanna know something else?

FIRST KISSES

MARY. Sure.

JOHN. I'm a virgin.

MARY. *(Where did that come from?)* What?

JOHN. You heard me. I'm a twenty-one-year-old-goddamned virgin. Remember? We used to talk about that when we were kids. We thought it'd be a good idea waiting for that perfect someone. *(A beat.)* What a load of bull horse that was. I shudda grabbed me some first chance I had.

MARY. You don't mean that.

JOHN. What about you?

MARY. What about me?

JOHN. Are you still a goddamned horse bull horse virgin too?

MARY. That's none of your business.

JOHN. *(Singsong.)* Ma-ry's a vir-gin. Ma-ry's a vir-gin.

MARY. *(Thumping him on his head.)* Stop that.

JOHN. Ow! So what are you waiting for?

MARY. *(Softly.)* That perfect someone.

JOHN

Me too I guess. 'Though I shudda grabbed me some while I had the chance.

MARY. Go to sleep.

JOHN. I'm not tired. I'm just gonna close my eyes for a minute because my eyes feel funny like they're going to fall out.

MARY. You do that.

JOHN. What, let my eyes fall out?

MARY. Shh.

JOHN. *(As he drifts off to sleep.)* Ma-ry's a vir-gin. Ma-ry's a vir-gin.

MARY. *(Stroking his head; speaks to the audience.)* I should have just stepped aside. I should have left town. I think Ellen and I both knew there was a... a conflict of interest when John insisted I be his best man. She picked out my dress. I wanted a tux. *(Big sigh.)*

FIRST KISSES

I am feeling so guilty right now... and so relieved. I didn't want him to marry her. I don't think I want him to marry anybody. *(Looking down at him.)* He's such a sweet little drunk. He slept for about an hour.

JOHN. *(Eyes still shut.)* Where am I?

MARY. Right here.

JOHN. I'm going to open my eyes now. *(Opens his eyes.)* I've never known light to hurt before.

MARY. My papa said he always got a headache whenever he drank champagne.

JOHN. What champagne? *(Sits up.)* I'm sorry.

MARY. What for?

JOHN. I don't know. We can start with that dress and work our way down. *(A beat.)* Why wouldn't she marry me?

MARY. Don't you remember what she said?

JOHN. Yes. She said that I loved you.

MARY. Do you?

JOHN. Sure! You're my best friend.

MARY. *(Standing.)* Great!

JOHN. Well, what's wrong with that?

MARY. Nothing pal.

JOHN. What's that about?

MARY. Buddy. Chum.

JOHN. C'mon. My head hurts enough without you giving me a hard time.

MARY. Sorry Amigo.

JOHN. All right! *(A beat.)* Was she right?

MARY. You're asking me?

JOHN. Yes.

MARY. *(Sitting.)* Do you love her?

JOHN. Yes.

MARY. Then why aren't you with her?

FIRST KISSES

JOHN. Good question.

MARY. Do you really love her?

JOHN. I don't know. I thought I did. *(Holding his head.)* Ow. Confusion makes my head hurt.

MARY. Maybe you just need to play the field some more. Date lots of other girls.

JOHN. I don't know. I don't think I'm much on dating.

MARY. How did you start dating Ellen?

JOHN. A bunch of us went out. One thing led to another. Why can't things be easy like with you and me?

MARY. We're easy?

JOHN. Sure. With you I never had to worry about date stuff 'cause we never dated.

MARY. We never did, did we?

JOHN. No, we just sort of hung out together.

MARY. We're best friends.

JOHN. Exactly.

MARY. And best friends don't date.

JOHN. They hang.

MARY. *(Getting up.)* Then I don't think I want to be best friends anymore.

JOHN. What are you talking about?

MARY. Never mind. Forget it.

(Turns away.)

JOHN. *(Getting up.)* Okay. You think I never thought about us?

MARY. What do you mean 'us'?

JOHN. Us. You and me. 'Ol buddy pal chum and amigo.

MARY. *(Turns towards JOHN, arms folded.)* Why didn't you ever say anything?

JOHN. Well why do you think?

MARY. I don't know!

JOHN. Then tell me why you never said anything.

MARY. What was I supposed to say?

JOHN. What was I supposed to say?

MARY. *(Turning.)* This isn't getting us anywhere.

JOHN. And that's why I never said anything. *(Walks to her, turns her around and holds onto her by the shoulders.)* Do you think I wanted to take the chance of losing the best friend I ever had?

MARY. So that's why you were about to marry someone else. To keep from losing me?

JOHN. Yes! You finally see the logic! *(No she doesn't, and neither does he.)* Wait a sec. That didn't sound the same out loud as it did in my head. The point I'm trying to make is that I do love you.

MARY. I know. As a friend.

JOHN. Not just a friend. A best friend.

MARY. *(She slumps- not again.)* I'm going home now. *(Turns to exit s.r.)*

JOHN. Cut me some slack, will you?

MARY. *(Stopping.)* Why?

JOHN. Because if I had said that I love you and I wanted us to be more than best friends - what would have happened if you didn't feel the same way? I'd have lost you and I wasn't ready to take that chance! *(Sitting back down on the porch.)* Do you know what I'm talking about?

MARY. *(Turning; agreeing.)* Oh yeah!

JOHN. Good, then explain it to me because I don't have any idea what the hell I just said.

MARY. So, how did you and Ellen ever get engaged anyway? Did she ask you?

JOHN. *(Thinking.)* I don't know. It just sort of happened.

MARY. It just sort of happened.

JOHN. Yeah.

FIRST KISSES

MARY. Things just sort of happen for you, don't they?

JOHN. What do you want from me?

MARY. You should have asked me!

JOHN. Asked you what? If you wanted to get married?

MARY. Yea-eah.

JOHN. What part of scared don't you understand?! Why didn't you ever ask me?

MARY. Because that's the part of scared that I understand!

JOHN. *(Quieter.)* What a pair of pathetic losers we are. *(A beat.)* So where do we go from here?

MARY. *(Walking towards him, and he to her.)* I don't know. So do you?

JOHN. Do I what?

MARY. Do you want to get married... someday.

JOHN. To you? *(She nods.)* I'd rather eat worms. *(She smiles.)* Are you really asking me to marry you?

MARY. Yes, I guess I am.

JOHN. Then shouldn't you be on one knee or something?

MARY. Oh, you want the traditional proposal.

JOHN. Yes. Yes I think I do. You'll have to ask my parent's permission, of course.

MARY. Of course. And of course my mother will have to approve of your dowry.

JOHN. Of course. *(A beat.)* How many kids are we talkin' here? I have my figure to worry about.

MARY. I don't know. Start at one and go from there?

JOHN. See? I knew you would say that.

MARY. I knew that you knew that I'd say that. *(A beat.)* So?

JOHN. So what?

MARY. You never answered me. Will you marry me?

JOHN. *(Stands, looks straight into her eyes, then without losing eye contact, gets down on one knee.)* Only if you'll... only if you'll really... I can't think of anything clever to say here.

MARY. Nothing's coming to me either.

JOHN. *(Standing.)* Then it's a deal. On three then. One... two... *(They lean in as they appear ready to kiss,when they both spit on their palms and shake hands.)* Three!

MARY. No going back on it now!

JOHN. Congratulations.

MARY. Thanks. But-

JOHN. But what?

MARY. But what about Ellen?

JOHN. What about her?

MARY. What if someday she decides she wants you back.

JOHN. *(Shaking his head.)* She won't. She knew. She knew even when I was afraid to admit it myself.

MARY. Do you... did you love her?

JOHN. Yes. But not like I love you. There was something missing.

MARY. What was that?

JOHN. She was never my best friend.

MARY. *(Smiling and pleased.)* And that would be me.

JOHN. That would be you.

MARY. And you.

JOHN. And me. *(A beat.)* Oh yeah. One more thing I probably should have mentioned earlier, but didn't.

MARY. What's that?

JOHN. You kept calling her Ellen, but her name is Helen.

MARY. *(Slaps him on the shoulder.)* You rat! You told me her name was Ellen! No wonder she never liked m... wa-ait a minute. No it's not.

JOHN. Yeah it is.

MARY. Not. I saw the wedding invitations.

JOHN. You saw your wedding invitation.

MARY. The newspaper engagement announcement?

JOHN. Dummied copy. It cost a day's pay, but was well worth it.

MARY. Our mutual friends?

JOHN. All in on it.

MARY. I'd be really really really angry with you right now if I weren't so gosh darn impressed. *(A beat.)* So what's next?

JOHN. We really really really need to get you out of that dress.

MARY. Why John, I'm blushing. Is that another proposal?

JOHN. Not at all. You really do look awful in that dress.

MARY. Too bad. *(She walks behind the shack and brings out a rolled up sleeping bag.)* You see, I lied. I did come here to take advantage of you.

JOHN. You hussy! I'm starting to have second thoughts about you.

MARY. I'm having some thoughts of my own.

JOHN. I don't know what to think of those thoughts.

MARY. *(As they lean in to kiss.)* Then... don't... think...

JOHN. I think I love you.

MARY. Okay... think that...

(They kiss as...)

End of Scene

Scene Two

(It is eleven years and eleven months later. JOHN and MARY are now 32 years old. It is a Saturday in May and about six thirty in the morning. The flowers are blooming on both small graves.)

NARRATOR. *(O.S.)* Do the best that you can just to get through the day. You talk to one 'nother, do you hear what they say? Do you hear what you say? Do you listen at all? Do you read between lines when you shouldn't at all? When did we stop list'ning? Was it gradual or fast? Eleven years older, a May morning will pass. There's nothing heroic 'bout turning deaf ears, they stopped listening slowly... the time to know this... draws near.

(JOHN ENTERS, sitting on the far s.l. corner of the shed porch. He's wearing jeans, sneakers and a team sweatshirt and a team baseball style cap - different teams. MARY will enter soon after and sit at the far s.r. side of the shed porch. She will be wearing jeans, a light top and a spring jacket and sneakers. They will not address or acknowledge each other during this scene. All action and dialogue will be directed to the audience.)

JOHN. I'm only thirty-two years old, so I know this isn't any kind of a mid-life crisis. And I know having a seven-year-old, a five-year-old and two-year-old can take the spark out of any marriage. Take now for instance. The kids are at their grandparents' for the weekend. My mom and dad and Mary's mom. Three grandparents, three kids... sounds fair to me. So what are we doing this weekend while we're alone?

MARY. *(ENTERS from s.r.)* Well, the first load of laundry is done. And I've got the second load started. I thought I'd take a break and watch the sun come up. It's supposed to be a nice day. Maybe I can hang the laundry out on the line instead of using the dryer.

FIRST KISSES

JOHN. I thought a nice romantic dinner for two, maybe a movie, a couple of drinks after, then a motel. Maybe a cheap motel. We could pay in cash and register as mister and misses Smith. Or else a nice hotel in the city. Room service. Breakfast in bed so we wouldn't have to get out of bed.

MARY. I didn't want to get out of bed this morning, but I have so much to do. And with the kids at their grandparents'—

JOHN. —this would be the perfect time to concentrate on us for a change.

MARY. —this would be the perfect time to get caught up on all the work that needs to get done.

JOHN. Then we'd come home from the hotel well rested and feel like getting some stuff done around here. Not as much, but some.

MARY. Laundry first, then the dishes - they've been piling up for about a week.

JOHN. I can finish putting the gas grill together and still have time for a rendezvous in the afternoon.

MARY. I'm embarrassed to have anyone look at my bathroom.

JOHN. But no, she said she had better things to do.

MARY. John was hoping for some kind of a romantic weekend. I said I'd like to, but there's so much to do here that I wouldn't be able to enjoy myself.

JOHN. *(Shrugging.)* She said she wouldn't enjoy it anyway.

MARY. But maybe a rain check. Okay? He just shrugged.

JOHN. Well, it's supposed to be a nice day today. I can weed the garden and other fun stuff.

MARY. I already miss the kids. I love them all.

JOHN. I love those kids. They make me laugh.

MARY. John is so good with them.

JOHN. Mary's the best mom.

JOHN.	MARY.
I just love those kids.	I just love those kids.

FIRST KISSES

MARY. *(A beat.)* It might be just me but John was acting kind of funny the other day.

JOHN. It's not that sex is the most important thing in the world-

MARY. He used to be happy just to hold me once in a while-

JOHN. But after a couple of weeks-

MARY. It's not that it's the most important thing in the world-

JOHN. And then after about a month-

MARY. It's just been different lately.

JOHN. After a month, it takes on a special... significance.

MARY. It's like he's forgotten how to be tender.

JOHN. Then when you get the chance, you gotta strike while the iron's hot.

MARY. Even when I want to start something, I remember how it was the last time.

JOHN. When was the last time?

MARY. And I'm just not up for it.

JOHN. Maybe I'll get a pocket calendar for my night table to keep track.

MARY. He's just been so perfunctory.

JOHN. That way I can tell her "Come on! It's been three weeks and four days already!"

MARY. I remember when he just liked to hold me.

JOHN. I'd settle for just holding her - just so I know she still cares.

MARY. I think I still look pretty good.

JOHN. I'm getting a bit of a belly, but overall I haven't changed much.

MARY. He looks as good as he did when we were married.

JOHN. She hasn't changed since college. Boy am I lucky. I wonder why she doesn't care?

MARY. Doesn't he know I still care?

JOHN. I got a phone call the other day.

FIRST KISSES

MARY. Did I mention I thought he was acting funny the other day?

JOHN. It was from Helen.

MARY. I mean, he's always bugging me about having lunch with him sometime. I like to use my lunch time to check on Ryan at day care, or meet with a teacher at school.

JOHN. She wanted to know if I was free for lunch.

MARY. I guess I shouldn't say he was bugging me. Of course I'd like to have lunch with him sometime.

JOHN. Now. Would it be inappropriate for me to meet my ex fiancé for lunch?

MARY. So I thought why not, and I called him up. His line was busy so I left voice mail.

JOHN. So would it be? Inappropriate I mean. Why would it be? It's just two old friends catching up. It's not like we were going to do anything. Just talk.

MARY. I had hoped he'd get the message.

JOHN. Okay. Helen and I were in love once. But we were just kids. What did we know from love? No, it'd be okay. Just catching up. Over lunch. *(Beat.)* I can rationalize almost anything if I put my mind to it.

MARY. I thought it'd be nice. We could catch up. We hardly ever see each other any more just to talk.

JOHN. So it's settled. It's not inappropriate. Did I mention we were meeting at her hotel restaurant?

MARY. He didn't call back right away, even though he always does. So I called again. Someone else picked up his line. He said John took an early lunch.

JOHN. I left early for lunch to give me plenty of time to pace and be nervous. What was I feeling guilty - I mean nervous - about? I wasn't doing anything wrong. It was just lunch. Why are my palms sweating?

MARY. He never goes out for lunch. He always eats in. Always.

JOHN. It's not like I'm meeting her for an affair.

(Nervous laughter.)

MARY. Unless he's meeting me somewhere for lunch.

JOHN. I could never have an affair.

MARY. Unless he's meeting someone else for lunch.

JOHN. I mean, she'd know. She'd know if I was having an affair.

MARY. Who could he have been meeting?

JOHN. So I finally went inside. Just two friends, right? God she was gorgeous.

MARY. All I know is, he wasn't having lunch with me.

JOHN. We talked for something like two hours.

MARY. I kept calling - he never answered. Over two hours...

JOHN. Helen still wasn't married. Can you believe that? Just hadn't found that right someone yet.

MARY. So at the end of the day, as I picked up the kids from daycare, it was my turn, one of our friends who was there picking up her daughter said to me that she saw John at the hotel downtown having lunch... with a pretty woman. I told her it was a family friend.

JOHN. Talking to your ex fiancé about your marital problems was probably a real dumb thing to do.

MARY. So what do I do?

JOHN. Helen said she knew someone with the same type of problems. Turned out that guy's wife was having an affair.

MARY. I mean, it's not like he's having an affair.

JOHN. Mary? Having an affair? Nonsense!

MARY. Nonsense.

JOHN. It's not that she couldn't. She's beautiful and sexy.

FIRST KISSES

MARY. She had to say it was a pretty woman he was sitting with.

JOHN.	MARY.
I just can't picture	I just can't picture
her having an affair.	him having an affair.
(A beat.)	*(A beat.)*
But it would explain a	But it would explain a
lot.	lot.
(A beat; dismissing	*(A beat; dismissing*
the thought.)	*the thought.)*
Noooo.	Noooo.

JOHN. So we had a real nice talk and that was it. She did say she was going to be in town one more day. Could we do this again tomorrow and I said sure. So meanwhile, I'm an above board kind of guy, right?

MARY. So do I ask him about it or do I wait for him to tell me. If I ask him, no matter how I ask him, I'm going to come off like I'm spying on him. Like I don't trust him, and of course I trust him.

JOHN. She trusts me. I can tell her the truth. It's no big deal. What's she going to do? Forbid it? On the other hand, maybe it would bother her that I met with Helen. I don't want her to feel bad. So, I'll tell her later, after Helen's gone. That way she won't feel so bad. Like I said, I can rationalize just about anything.

MARY. If he doesn't mention anything then there was nothing to mention. Right?

JOHN. I wanted to make love with Mary that night. She wasn't in the mood.

MARY. If he had brought me flowers, then I would have known.

JOHN. I bought flowers. Then when I got to about a hundred feet from home... red flags, sirens, bells, whistles. I pitched the posies.

MARY. So that night I asked if he wanted to do lunch the next day.

JOHN. I told her I couldn't. It just wasn't a good day. Probably next week though.

MARY. He was meeting her again.

JOHN. I didn't lie-

MARY. So do I bump into them tomorrow?

JOHN. Why did I feel like I was sneaking around? I wasn't sneaking around. And let's face it, it's pretty egotistical of me to think Helen wants anything but lunch.

MARY. I called the next day. He left early for lunch.

JOHN. I got to the hotel restaurant and got a message to meet her in her room. She was probably just running late and didn't want me to wait alone in the restaurant. Or am I rationalizing?

MARY. I got to the hotel and saw him get into an elevator.

JOHN. I got into the elevator and thought what am I doing?

MARY. What was he doing? I sat down in one of the chairs in the lobby, staring at the elevator door, trying my damnedest not to cry. What have I done?

JOHN. I got off the elevator and went to her room.

MARY. I couldn't move.

JOHN. I almost didn't knock on the door. But I did.

MARY. I was counting the minutes. Two so far.

JOHN. Well, it turns out she did want a... relationship.

MARY. Three minutes.

JOHN. I looked at her and she was beautiful.

MARY. Four minutes.

JOHN. And I said I want you.

MARY. Five.

JOHN. But I can't.

MARY. Six.

JOHN. She said Mary would never know. I said I would know. I've never lied to her before and I couldn't start now.

FIRST KISSES

MARY. Seven.

JOHN. I apologized and started to leave. She took my arm and when I turned around, she was crying.

MARY. Eight.

JOHN. She said she knew I wouldn't. That she still loved me. She kissed me on the cheek and we laughed as she wiped off the lipstick.

MARY. Twelve minutes. Then the elevator door opened and there he was! *(Quieter.)* There he was. Twelve minutes. Nothing could happen in only twelve minutes.

JOHN. Twelve minutes. That's got to be the fastest non-affair on record.

MARY. So I stood there like an idiot, when it hit me... I can't let him see me here. So I sat down and put up a newspaper in front of my face. How embarrassing.

JOHN. I walked outside the hotel and felt... I don't know how I felt. Embarrassed. Proud. Guilty. Definitely guilty. But mostly what I felt was sad.

MARY. I felt happy and sad all at once.

JOHN	MARY
How did I ever let it get this far? I got out my phone and called. Voice mail. I left a message...	How did I ever let it get this far? I got out my phone and called. Voice mail. I left a message...

End of Scene

Scene Three

(It is ten years, three months later in mid-August, JOHN and MARY are about to turn forty three years old. The shed is still there, as are the flowers. It is almost noontime on a Saturday.)

NARRATOR. *(O.S.)* They are now in their forties these heroes of ours, with three teenage children to whittle the hours. Ten years ago — easy compared with today? So where are they heading? They must still lead the way. Warm August breezes, some late summer showers, loving those not yet grown up... they are our summer flowers.

(JOHN runs on dressed in a T-shirt, shorts and sneakers and no socks. MARY soon follows wearing a tank top, jean shorts and sneakers with ankle socks. JOHN is clearly agitated and MARY is clearly enjoying it.)

JOHN. Where is she? I know she comes out here! I'm gonna lock her up, that's what I'm gonna do! She won't see the light of day for twenty years!

MARY. *(Trying not to laugh.)* Take it easy! It's not the end of the world!

JOHN. Oh yes it is. My world! *(Calling out.)* Jessica! Where are you? You can run but you can't hide!

MARY. She's not hiding. She doesn't even know you're looking for her.

JOHN. She will when I find her by God!

MARY. I think she's over at Dawn's house working on an English paper or something.

JOHN. You think?! You think you know where our daughter is? You don't know?

MARY. You don't know where she is either.

JOHN. Don't you take her side on this!

MARY. I'm not taking anybody's side. *(Taking him by the arm and gently maneuvering him to sit down on the porch.)* Come and sit down. *(He sits.)* Relax. She's at Dawn's.

JOHN. *(Standing.)* But how do we know she's at Dawn's? How can we be sure?

MARY. You're acting like such a father.

JOHN. Because that's what I am. A father. And Jessie's my daughter. A daughter who lives only to break her father's heart.

MARY. *(Sitting him down.)* If you weren't snooping where you didn't belong—

JOHN. *(Standing.)* I was not snooping. Don't say I was snooping when I wasn't snooping because I wasn't.

MARY. Snooping.

JOHN. Darn right I wasn't.

MARY. Then what were you doing going through her dresser drawers.

JOHN. I was helping you put away the laundry!

MARY. A likely story.

JOHN. Don't you poke fun at me! This is not to be poked fun at!

MARY. Of course not.

JOHN. I didn't go looking for trouble.

MARY. Of course you didn't.

JOHN. I just happened to find it.

MARY. Of course you did.

JOHN. You're humoring me, aren't you?

MARY. Of course I am. *(Standing, facing him, putting her arms around his neck and shoulders.)* We'll talk to her calmly. Respectfully. Like she's an adult.

JOHN. Sixteen is not an adult. Sixteen is a little girl child.

MARY. Sixteen is old enough to have a condom in her sock drawer.

JOHN. *(Breaking away.)* Shh! Don't say that awful word!

MARY. Condom. *(A beat.)* Condom condom condom.

JOHN. How can you make fun of this? Aren't you worried about it?

MARY. I'd be more worried if she weren't using them.

JOHN. *(Gasps.)* Oh my God! You don't really believe she's not using them do you?

MARY. Make up your mind, will you. Either you want her to use 'em or you don't.

JOHN. Just how active is she?

MARY. Active?

JOHN. You know, *(Whispering.)* sexually *(Aloud.)* active.

MARY. You can ask her later.

JOHN. Me?! Why should I be the one to ask her?

MARY. Because you're the one who wants to know.

JOHN. I don't want to know that!

MARY. You're losing me.

JOHN. I want to know what this was doing in her sock drawer.

MARY. Oh that. What kind is it? Here, let me look. *(Takes condom from him and reads the wrapper.)* "'Gladiator' brand condom." Oh look, it's got the word "glad" underlined.

JOHN. You're taking this far too lightly you know.

MARY. *(Continuing.)* "Made with the highest quality material available..."

JOHN. Who's she using it with, that's what I'd like to know.

MARY. "Thin enough for his pleasure..."

JOHN. Whoever he is, he better keep his 'pleasure' to himself.

MARY. "... with extra ribbing to enhance her enjoyment."

JOHN. Her 'enjoyment'? Her 'enjoyment'? She's not supposed to 'enjoy' anything!

FIRST KISSES

MARY. That explains a lot.

JOHN. Especially 'ribbed'! How old is he? Twenty one? If he's twenty one we can have him sent to jail.

MARY. Oh John, please—

JOHN. A couple of months in the big house will make him re-think what a 'gladiator' is!

MARY. *(Laughing.)* John stop it. I have to tell you. I gave her the condom.

JOHN. You?

MARY. We were having a long talk about, you know, *(Whispers.)* sex, *(Aloud.)* when she asked about condoms, so I took one of yours and gave it to her.

JOHN. You gave it to her? Why didn't you tell me?

MARY. I promised I wouldn't. It's a little embarrassing you know.

JOHN. I suppose. But why didn't you tell me when I first found it.

MARY. Oh you were being far too entertaining to say anything.

JOHN. *(Sighs.)* She's growing up so fast. And she's so beautiful.

MARY. Yes she is.

JOHN. She looks like you.

MARY. So they say.

JOHN. Things have changed since we were growing up.

MARY. You think so? I don't.

JOHN. No?

MARY. Kids are kids.

JOHN. That's very profound.

MARY. I know.

JOHN. You're a good mother.

MARY. Thank you.

JOHN. But did you have to give her a rubber?

FIRST KISSES

MARY. Actually I gave her two. One was to keep.

JOHN. What was the other one for?

MARY. Demonstrational purposes. When we finished, we blew it up like a balloon.

JOHN. So she knows what they're for?

MARY. Afraid so. Come on! We both talked to the kids years ago about this. She's known since she was ten.

JOHN. Ten? Was she only ten?

MARY. We knew when we were ten. So now they know. What's the difference?

JOHN. I was a mature ten.

MARY. You aren't a mature forty-three.

JOHN. *(Laughing.)* Remember when we were ten? Or eleven?

MARY. And my folks just got through giving me 'the talk'.

JOHN. And the two of us went for a walk.

MARY. Do you remember what you said when I told you about it? *(JOHN starts to act even more embarrassed.)* Do you?

JOHN. Yes. I asked you if it was all true.

MARY. I couldn't believe you asked that.

JOHN. Well, you've got to admit that the whole thing is pretty far fetched.

MARY. If you say so..

JOHN. So I guess I better put this back.

MARY. And keep your yap shut.

JOHN. I don't know why she needs one. You didn't have one at her age. Did you?

MARY. Sure. I had one 'just in case' when I was sixteen.

JOHN. You carried around a rubber with you when you were sixteen? Get out!

MARY. Why do you find that so hard to believe?

JOHN. Because you never said anything to me about it, and you told me everything.

FIRST KISSES

MARY. Well I wasn't about to flash a rubber in front of you.

JOHN. Why not?

MARY. What would have happened if I, a sixteen year old girl, had shown you, a sixteen year old boy, that I had my very own condom?

JOHN. *(Agreeing with her.)* I'd have started to stutter like the village idiot. You were very wise.

MARY. I still am.

JOHN. Of course, if I had known you were such a slut, I'd have put the moves to you a lot sooner than I did.

MARY. You put the moves to me?

JOHN. That's not how you remember it?

MARY. That's not how it happened.

JOHN. So what else haven't you told me?

MARY. Nothing.

JOHN. By 'nothing' do you mean 'nothing' or by 'nothing' do you mean 'something'.

MARY. Nothing.

JOHN. So I'm up to date on everything?

MARY. I guess.

JOHN. No more surprises?

MARY. I guess not.

JOHN. I just thought of something.

MARY. What?

JOHN. That condom you used to carry around with you.

MARY. Yes?

JOHN. Was that the one we used when we first...

MARY. That was the one.

JOHN. The one you had since you were sixteen.

MARY. Yep.

JOHN. The one we didn't use until we were twenty-one.

MARY. What a memory you have.

JOHN. Y-you mean we had s-s-sex using a f-f-five year old c-c-c-c-c-rubber?

MARY. You're s-stuttering.

JOHN. It was five years old!

MARY. So? It wasn't like it got worn out over time or anything.

JOHN. (holds up the condom to her)Do you see these numbers here?

MARY. Yes.

JOHN. Do you know what they are?

MARY. Serial numbers?

JOHN. No, they would be the expiration date!

MARY. Condoms expire?

JOHN. Yes!

MARY. Well I'll be. Who knew?

JOHN. I knew! Does Jessica knew?

MARY. I suppose I should tell her.

JOHN. That would be best.

MARY. Oh look here.

JOHN. What?

MARY. This expires tomorrow.

JOHN. Toss it.

MARY. It would be a shame to waste it.

JOHN. Nothing we can do about it. Can't take any chances you know.

MARY. I can think of one thing.

JOHN. What's that?

MARY. You are so thick sometimes.

JOHN. Then spell it out for me.

MARY. K-I-S-S.

(They kiss.)

JOHN. You're a good speller.

MARY. So. Would you like to go home and thumb through the entire dictionary?

JOHN. *(Arms around each other as they exit right.)* Literacy begins at home.

MARY. I thought you might think that.

JOHN. One thing still bothers me though.

MARY. What's that?

JOHN. When you stop and think about it...

MARY. Ye-e-e-s-s?

JOHN. Well, you do have to admit the whole thing is pretty far fetched.

MARY. You're telling me.

End of Scene

Scene Four

(It is ten years, ten months later. JOHN and MARY are now 52 years old. Their oldest son, Jeffery, is about twenty-seven years old while middle child Jessica is twenty-five and youngest Ryan is twenty-two. It is an early Monday morning. There is a porch swing, or glider, on the porch.)

NARRATOR. *(O.S.)* Small heroes grow upwards, much to cha-grins, and amusements therein. And awe. Take pride as they do, even tho' we had nothing to do with the fact that they grow... or grew. All at once on their own, all at once on our own- Just the fact they're... we're together, is proof we're the same after all.)

(MARY jogs on from s.r. She is wearing a jogging suit complete with high priced shoes, sweatband and wrist bands. She may have just a touch of gray. She jogs to center stage and continues jogging in place.)

MARY. *(Calling off right.)* Come on slowpoke! We have to keep our heart rate at the optimum or these workouts won't mean a thing! *(Looking around.)* What a beautiful June morning!

(JOHN ENTERS from right. He is dragging his heels, and slumping. His sweat suit is soaked with sweat. He makes it to the edge of the porch and collapses.)

JOHN. My optimum heart rate just flat lined.

MARY. *(Looking at her watch.)* Okay, that's time. *(She stops jogging and starts walking, stretching and shaking out.)* You're only as young as you feel.

JOHN. You keep saying that as though you mean it.

MARY. That's because I mean it. I feel young. I am young.

JOHN. No you're not.

MARY. I beg your pardon?

JOHN. *(Shaking his head.)* We're fifty-two. We're not young anymore.

MARY. Speak for yourself.

JOHN. Nothing I can do about it. It's official.

MARY. How is it 'official'?

JOHN. Tell me... what radio station do you listen to?

MARY. You know the one, the one that plays the songs I like.

JOHN. What songs do you like?

MARY. The ones I listen to.

JOHN. Where?

MARY. On the radio.

JOHN. What station.

MARY. *(Relents.)* The oldies.

JOHN. Could you say that a little louder please?

MARY. Why? Are you 'deef'?

JOHN. No. We need it once more just for the record.

MARY. *(Loudly.)* The oldies.

JOHN. A-ha!

MARY. Save your a-ha's.

JOHN. You listen to the oldies station. You listen to oldies so that makes you an oldie.

MARY. That does not make me an oldie. I listen to that station because most of the new music nowadays is crap.

JOHN. That's the official slogan of an oldie.

MARY. It is not.

JOHN. *(Singing.)* Oh beau-oo-tiful for oldies songs-

MARY. Stop it.

JOHN. That's the oldies anthem.

MARY. It is not.

JOHN. *(Continues singing.)* While eating healthy bran-

MARY. I'm not listening.

JOHN. *(Continues singing.)* While meas-ur-ing cho-les-terol-

MARY. *(Looking around.)* Where's a stick? I need a really big stick!

JOHN. *(Still singing)* Our heart rates we will max-

MARY. "Max" and "bran" don't rhyme.

JOHN. It's free verse.

MARY. It's not.

JOHN. I'm ahead of my time.

MARY. Enough! Music doesn't define your youth. It defines

your taste.

JOHN. And our taste is old.

MARY. Why are you so fixated on being old? *(Stretches a beat.)* Do you think I should dye my hair?

JOHN. Another color? Sure!

MARY. No just a little something to remove the gr... the lighter strands.

JOHN. You mean the gray?

MARY. I mean the lighter strands. I don't think you could call them a true gray.

JOHN. Anything lighter than black is gray.

MARY. I'll think about it.

JOHN. So why the big fitness craze over the last couple of months?

MARY. I've always exercised. On and off. It makes me feel good.

JOHN. Can't you feel good with a dish of ice cream?

MARY. Okay, enough idle chit chat. Race you to the shower!

(Runs off right.)

JOHN. *(Calling off.)* I'll give you a head start. *(To the audience.)* All this exercise can't possibly be good for you. At first I thought maybe she was seeing someone else. Crazier things have happened. But the thing is, she's been making a lot of passes at me. Mind you, I'm not complaining. It just makes me wonder what's gotten into her lately. *(Stands.)* Well, I'll figure it out sooner or later. *(Stretching.)* I may be slow, but I catch on eventually. *(Stretches a beat.)* Hey, did I mention we're going to be grandparents? How 'bout that huh? Our oldest, Jeff, and his wife Angie are having their first any day now. The car's all gassed up for the three hour drive. *(Starts jogging in place.)* We can't wait! All the fun and none of the bother.

Being a granddad is going to be great! *(He jogs off right, then after a couple beats, jogs on backwards, stops, and continues to address the audience.)* I've just put my finger on it, haven't I? *(Sighs.)* It was better walking around in ignorant bliss, because no matter what I do or say now, it'll be wrong. I'm taking the long way home. *(Jogs off left.)*

(MARY ENTER from right, wearing her office work clothes. She addresses the audience.)

MARY. Where'd he go? Have you seen him? I haven't seen him since this morning and it's *(Looking at her watch.)* about four o'clock now. So I'm at work, right? And someone sends me flowers, okay? "For me?" I says. And you know how it is, flowers are delivered at work, everyone crowds around, "Did John send those?" "Isn't he something?" Stuff like that. So I read the card with everyone crowded around. *(She holds up the card and reads it.)* "Grandma, you're as young as you feel.", signed Grandpa. Now everyone knows! *(Looking around.)* Maybe he's at the house. *(Calls off right as she EXITS.)* Where are you *(Menacingly.)* Gr-randpa?

(JOHN ENTERS from left. He wearing nice, not dressy pants and polo shirt. He is also wearing a light jacket, as it is early evening. He addresses the audience.)

JOHN. Have you seen her lately? I called and left a message that I wanted to take her out to dinner. *(He looks at his watch.)* I made reservations for six and it's five-thirty now. I know, I know... too little too late. 'Grandma'. What was I thinking! *(Suddenly.)* What if someone says something about her gray hairs?! What if I just move to Siberia now before winter sets in. *(Looks at his watch again.)* She's not in the house, and she's not here. I don't know, maybe she went for a jog. *(Starts to go left when...)*

MARY. *(Calling from off right.)* John!

JOHN. *(Stopping in his tracks.)* I don't know if I like the sound of that.

MARY. *(ENTERS from right. She is wearing a calf length dress coat.)* Is that what you're wearing to dinner?

JOHN. Yes?

MARY. I don't think so. Where we're going requires a jacket and tie.

JOHN. And a credit card?

MARY. A platinum credit card. Maybe two, I'm hungry.

JOHN. Where are we going?

MARY. To the Rosewood Inn. I made reservations.

JOHN. To the Rosewood Inn? Do you have any idea how much- *(Sees MARY glaring at him.)* The Rosewood Inn sounds lovely.

MARY. Good, I'm glad. Now go change.

JOHN. *(Crosses right.)* The Rosewood Inn. We haven't been there in, what, four, five years? Do they still have the dance bands there during the summer?

MARY. Indeed they do.

JOHN. We can't stay out too late dancing you know. We both have to work in the morning.

MARY. I don't care.

JOHN. You'll care when the alarm clock goes off.

MARY. Maybe I won't set the alarm clock.

JOHN. What's gotten into you lately?

MARY. Nothing.

JOHN. Hey, did you dye your hair?

MARY. No.

JOHN. Yes you did. It's darker.

MARY. It's the same color it's always been. Only more so.

JOHN. So much for growing old gracefully.

FIRST KISSES

MARY. I don't want to grow old gracefully.

JOHN. How do you want to grow old?

MARY. Under protest.

JOHN. *(Walking towards her.)* Come on! You don't need to worry about getting old. You look great.

MARY. You mean for my age? Because if you mean for my age I'm kicking you so hard all the Viagra in the world won't help.

JOHN. No you look great.

MARY. For a grandmother? If you mean for a grandmother then I'm using the other foot.

JOHN. *(Laughing.)* No, you look great! *(A beat.)* So that is what this is all about.

MARY. What what's all about?

JOHN. Everything. The exercise. The hair.

MARY. It's not fair! I don't feel any different than I did ten years ago.

JOHN. So? Neither do I.

MARY. Something inside keeps telling me that I'm younger than what the calendar says I am. I don't want to be told I can't dance 'til two in the morning. Or I can't still play my music loud.

JOHN. No one's telling you you can't.

MARY. And I don't want to worry about if I eat this then I'll have gas or I can't eat that because my arteries will harden.

JOHN. I hate it when that happens.

MARY. And I want construction workers to yell rude and obscene things when I walk by.

JOHN. Believe me, that's not all it's cracked up to be.

MARY. And look at you!

JOHN. What about me?

MARY. You look really good... for your age.

JOHN. G'wan! You're just saying that.

MARY. Am I overreacting to all this?

FIRST KISSES

JOHN. I don't know. Maybe you're pre-menopausal.

MARY. *(Laughing and hitting him on the arm.)* Don't even joke about that.

JOHN. *(Also laughing.)* Ow! Okay, okay! *(A beat.)* You really, really look good for an old broad.

MARY. Really? Am I still a broad?

JOHN. You betcha.

MARY. You are one sweet talkin' fool.

JOHN. You bring it out in me.

MARY. I guess I won't mind growing old as long as you do it with me.

JOHN. That's such a cliché. I guess you're just showing your age. *(JOHN's cell phone rings.)* Yyyyyellow! *(Listening.)* What? You are? She is? We are?

MARY. What? What?! Who is it? Is it Jeff? Is it Angie?!

JOHN. *(To MARY.)* It's Jeff. *(Into phone.)* What? A boy? *(To MARY.)* They had a boy. *(MARY lets out an excited scream.)* Seven pounds, six ounces. Black hair and lots of it.

MARY. *(Excited.)* It's a boy? Is it a boy? Are they sure? How can they tell?

JOHN. *(Deadpan.)* They rolled it on its back and looked.

MARY. *(Nodding in serious acknowledgment.)* Ah.

JOHN. *(Into phone.)* What? Okay, we'll see you in a few hours. *(Hangs up.)*

MARY. *(Yelling.)* A name- get a name!

JOHN. He hung up.

MARY. And you didn't get a name?

JOHN. Yes. His name is Clarence.

MARY. It is not!

JOHN. What's wrong with Clarence? My grandfather was named Clarence.

MARY. *(As just realizing.)* I'm a grandma!

FIRST KISSES

JOHN. Yes you are.

MARY. I can't wait to tell everyone!(JOHN reacts very surprised at this) But it's not really Clarence.

JOHN. You'll know when we get there.

MARY. It is not Clarence.

JOHN. No sense in leaving now. Everyone will be asleep by the time we get there. So lets go out to dinner and dancing and celebrate!

MARY. Let's go home.

JOHN. Home? Don't you want to still go out?

MARY. If we go out, I'm afraid I'll catch cold.(she stands in front of JOHN, back facing down stage and opens her coat. We see from the expression on JOHN's face that she has nothing on underneath the coat.)So. Does this look like the body of a grandmother?

(closes her coat)

JOHN. N-n-not l-like any gr-gr-grandmother I know!

MARY. Then let's go old man!

JOHN. Wait.(JOHN embraces MARY and they kiss.)You're going to make a great grandma.

MARY. Please don't put the word 'great' in front of grandma! At least not for another thirty years!

JOHN. Oops. Sorry.

MARY. (playfully pushing him back)Race you home!(runs off s.r.)

JOHN. (as he runs off s.r. after her)Man she's quick for an old broad!

End of Scene

FIRST KISSES

Scene Five

(It is twenty years later and JOHN and MARY are now seventy-two
years old. The bench/swing is still on the porch, well taken care
of. It is October. A nice, pleasant Wednesday afternoon.)

NARRATOR. *(O.S.)* We see ahead twilight, we look back at
dawn- not so too far diff'rent, it's sunlight... that's all. One looking
one way, one looking the other- both meeting together as father and
mother. How many people do we meet on our journey? Our son and
our daughter... and the people before me. Each one takes a turn,
each one has a goal- a hero's reflection... simply love... don't you
know.

(JOHN and MARY enter from s.r., we see him pushing her along in
a wheel chair. They are dressed comfortably for fall. He is wear-
ing a hat. He pushes her to the s.r. corner of the shed and waits.)

JOHN. How's this?
MARY. For what?
JOHN. You wanted to come out here so here we are.
MARY. Here we are.
JOHN. So is this okay?
MARY. Where will you sit?
JOHN. I'll stand.
MARY. You'll get tired.
JOHN. No I won't.
MARY. If you say so.
JOHN. I say so. *(He hugs her around the shoulders from be-*
hind.) So is this okay?
MARY. No. I want you to sit next to me.
JOHN. I'm fine here.
MARY. Oh for... *(Gets up.)*

FIRST KISSES

JOHN. Easy! Easy! *(JOHN helps her as she walks to the bench to sit down.)*

MARY. I'm not an invalid you know.

JOHN. You had a heart attack.

MARY. That was days ago. It's ancient history by now. It's not like I died or anything.

JOHN. Your heart stopped.

MARY. And it's not like it didn't start up again. At least I think it did. Anyway, quit hovering over me. *(Sits.)*

JOHN. Quit joking. You were technically dead.

MARY. Not really. I still had brain waves which is more than I can say for you. Sit.

JOHN. *(Sitting.)* You've got to take it easy.

MARY. Oh, nonsense. The doctor says I'm fine.

JOHN. You're not fine. You're tired all the time.

MARY. Well duh. I just had a heart attack.

JOHN. Oh right, like I forgot.

MARY. Honey, in a few days I'll be getting my strength back and I'll slowly start my exercises and before you know it, I'll be as good as new.

JOHN. Don't push yourself.

MARY. I won't. *(They sit contentedly enjoying each other's silent company for bit.)* This is a rather pleasant day for October, isn't it?

JOHN. I think so.

MARY. A pleasant day. *(A beat.)* Oh I just remembered something.

JOHN. What's that, Love?

MARY. I never got around to planting those flower bulbs.

JOHN. Sure you did. Last week before your Timex took a lickin'.

MARY. Not the bulbs at home, the bulbs out here.

JOHN. We don't plant bulbs here Sweetheart. Remember? They're perennials. They come up on their own every year.

MARY. *(Laughing.)* Oh, that's right. I forgot. You don't know.

JOHN. Don't know what?

MARY. These flowers here. They don't come up every year.

JOHN. Sure they do. We've watched them come up every year.

MARY. Well, yes and no.

JOHN. Yes and no?

MARY. My Dear, every fall I've dug up the old bulbs and planted new ones to come up in the spring.

JOHN. I thought they were perennials. My mother said they would come up every year.

MARY. I can say it now. Your mother, may she rest in peace, was wrong.

JOHN. My mother was wrong?

MARY. May she rest in peace. *(A beat.)* I've got the bulbs in the house. You can help me plant them later.

JOHN. Okay, if you're sure.

MARY. I'm sure. I've been doing it for sixty years.

JOHN. Sixty years is a long time to take care of hamster graves.

MARY. Feeling old? I'm not. I'm just getting started.

JOHN. I've been in love with you for sixty years?

MARY. Give or take a year.

JOHN. Boy are you lucky!

MARY. Boy am I lucky?

JOHN. I'm glad you agree.

MARY. Why am I lucky but not you?

JOHN. Oh, I'm lucky too.

MARY. Good.

JOHN. Only not as lucky as you.

MARY. Egomaniac.

JOHN. Just the facts. *(A beat.)* Okay, I'm as lucky as you are.

MARY. I should hope so. *(A beat.)* Johnny?

JOHN. Yessy?

FIRST KISSES

MARY. If I should go before you-

JOHN. Where are you going?

MARY. No. If I should go before you.

JOHN. Oh! Don't. Let's not talk about that.

MARY. But if-

JOHN. No! We've already talked about it to death. *(Winces at what he just said.)* Our affairs are in order. We know who gets what where and when. Everybody knows! Everything's settled. So... don't.

MARY. But if I do go before you- *(JOHN throws up his arms.)* Just listen to me. *(JOHN starts to interrupt, but she cuts him off.)* Listen to me.

JOHN. Okay. I'm listening.

MARY. I want you to promise me something.

JOHN. Whatever it is I promise. There. Now we're done-

MARY. If I should go before you-

JOHN. -except she's still going!

MARY. I want you to promise me that you'll get married again.

JOHN. What?

MARY. I feel so much better now.

JOHN. Married again? I'm not getting married again. I haven't the strength.

MARY. I need to know you'll be taken care of when I'm gone.

JOHN. I can take care of myself. I'm taking care of you.

MARY. And you take care of me just fine. But you're not taking care of yourself.

JOHN. Okay, okay. I'll get married again. Happy?

MARY. Yes.

JOHN. Anything to shut you up. *(A beat)* Can she be younger?

MARY. She'd almost have to be.

JOHN. No, I mean really younger.

MARY. You're talking like sixty five or something?

JOHN. What would I want to hook up with a sixty five year old bat for? I mean younger.

MARY. How much younger?

JOHN. I would consider forty to be too old.

MARY. Then the answer is no.

JOHN. Too bad. You won't be here anyway.

MARY. I'll haunt you.

JOHN. I think she'll be twenty five. And blonde.

MARY. John, there isn't a twenty five year old blonde on this planet that will have you.

JOHN. Sour grapes. *(A beat.)* Thirty?

MARY. No. Nothing under sixty five.

JOHN. You never let me have any fun. *(They sit quietly for a bit.)* You'll never know you know.

MARY. I'm sorry I brought it up. *(A beat.)* Sixty years! You've really loved me for sixty years!

JOHN. I said so didn't I? So what about you?

MARY. What about me?

JOHN. Wouldn't you say you've been in love with me for sixty years?

MARY. Of course I would.

JOHN. Good.

MARY. On and off.

JOHN. Am I on now or off?

MARY. Oh, you're on now. Definitely on.

JOHN. Thank you.

MARY. So.

JOHN. So what?

MARY. So. You feeling lucky?

JOHN. Lucky? What do you mean lucky?

MARY. *(Snuggling.)* You know. Lucky.

JOHN. Oh! Why didn't you say so? Do you know someone?

MARY. You're off now.

FIRST KISSES

JOHN. Oh, you meant with you. Good God woman, you just had a heart attack. Do you want another?

MARY. Don't flatter yourself. I was just asking. You always say I never ask.

JOHN. Thank you for asking. *(A beat.)* So do you know someone?

MARY. Come here you. *(She pulls his face down and they enjoy a nice long kiss.)*

JOHN. Are you trying to give me a heart attack?

MARY. Mmmm. That was nice. Let's have another. *(They do.)*

JOHN. There isn't a twenty five year old blonde who's got a thing over you.

MARY. I know. *(A beat.)* The family's coming over tomorrow?

JOHN. Just for a little while. The doctor said it'd be okay just for a little while.

MARY. Oh, what does she know.

JOHN. For a little while. We'll see how you do.

MARY. Yes sir. *(A beat.)* When did you first know you loved me?

JOHN. That's easy. It was after my hamster died. You got me a new one. But you didn't go out and buy one. You gave me your own.

MARY. How'd you find that out?

JOHN. I overheard our mothers talking.

MARY. I can see it all as if it were yesterday.

JOHN. Wasn't it?

MARY. You know, when my heart stopped, I saw my papa.

JOHN. Did you?

MARY. Uh-huh. He was just as young and handsome as ever. And I was seventeen all over again. He said it wasn't my time yet, and won't be for quite a while.

JOHN. That's nice. Did he say anything about me?

MARY. Something about not taking any long trips.

JOHN. Ha ha. Funny.

MARY. I thought so.

JOHN. So when did you know you loved me?

MARY. When I saw you crying because your hamster had died. I just... knew. That's why I had to kiss you.

JOHN. Our first kiss.

MARY. Our first kiss.

JOHN. It was very nice.

MARY. It was.

JOHN. It was that second kiss. *(MARY starts laughing.)* When you stuck your tongue down the back of my throat. *(Shudders.)* I can still feel it. All wet and slimy.

MARY. You went looking for worms to eat.

JOHN. I had to get that taste out of my mouth. It's a wonder I could have a normal relationship with a girl after that.

MARY. Come here you.

JOHN. You're not going to do it again, are you?

MARY. You should be so lucky. *(They kiss.)* I'm a little tired. I'm going to take a nap here with you.

JOHN. Mary?

MARY. Yes, Love?

JOHN. This is just a nap right? Just a nap?

MARY. *(Gives him a peck on the cheek.)* Just a short nap, then I'll let you walk me home. *(She snuggles in, smiling and closes her eyes.)*

JOHN. *(Kissing her on top of her head, and stroking her hair.)* I remember that first kiss as vividly as the last. And all I ask for, all I ever want for the rest of my life, is your next kiss.

Curtain. End of Play